Health Facts

All About Your
Skin, Hair and Teeth

Donna Bailey

STECK-VAUGHN
LIBRARY
A Division of Steck-Vaughn Company

Austin, Texas

How to Use This Book

This book tells you many things about your skin, hair, and teeth. There is a Table of Contents on the next page. It shows you what each double page of the book is about. For example, pages 10 and 11 tell you about "What Skin Does."

On many of these pages you will find words that are printed in **bold** type. The bold type shows you that these words are in the Glossary on pages 46 and 47. The Glossary explains the meaning of some words that may be new to you.

At the very end of the book there is an Index. The Index tells you where to find certain words in the book. For example, you can use it to look up words like dermis, sebum, and keratin, and many other words to do with your skin, hair, and teeth.

Printed and bound in the United States
1 2 3 4 5 6 7 8 9 0 LB 95 94 93 92 91

Library of Congress Cataloging-in-Publication-Data

Bailey, Donna.
    All about your skin, hair, and teeth / Donna Bailey.
        p.   cm.—(Health facts)
    Rev. ed. of: Skin, hair, and teeth / Bridget: and Neil Ardley. 1988.
    Includes index.
    Summary: Describes the functions, characteristics, disorders, and care of skin, teeth, and hair.
    ISBN 0-8114-2783-8
    1. Skin—Juvenile literature.   2. Hair—Juvenile literature.   3. Teeth—Juvenile literature.
    [1. Skin.   2. Hair.   3. Teeth.]
    I. Ardley, Bridget. Skin, hair, and teeth.   II. Title.
    III. Series: Bailey, Donna. Health facts.
    QP88.5.B34   1990
    612.7'9—dc20   90-10050
                                                        CIPAC

Contents

Introduction

The way we look depends on our skin,
hair, and teeth.

Our skin forms a waterproof
covering which protects the insides
of our bodies. Our skin helps to keep
us cool when the weather is hot, and
warm when the weather is cold. It
keeps germs out of your body, too.

Chimpanzees and other animals have thick hair covering most of their bodies, but humans have very little hair.

The skin of a frog is always damp. A frog can drink and breathe through its skin. The different colors of frogs' skins help them to hide from their enemies.

the color of this tree frog makes it hard to see among the leaves

Finding Out

This painting shows Samson fast asleep, and his long hair being cut off to make him lose his strength.

A long time ago people thought that long hair gave them a lot of power. Egyptian kings wore wigs of gold and silver, and long beards to make them look important.

false teeth made 2,500 years ago in Italy

6

The photograph, taken under a **microscope,** shows the surface of the skin and a hair sticking up out of it. Scientists today can easily examine our skin and hair using a microscope.

Long ago, if someone had a toothache, the bad tooth was usually pulled out. People made false teeth from wood, ivory, gold, and silver to replace the missing teeth. The false teeth in the picture were made of ivory and then fixed to gold **bridges** which held them in place.

What Is Skin?

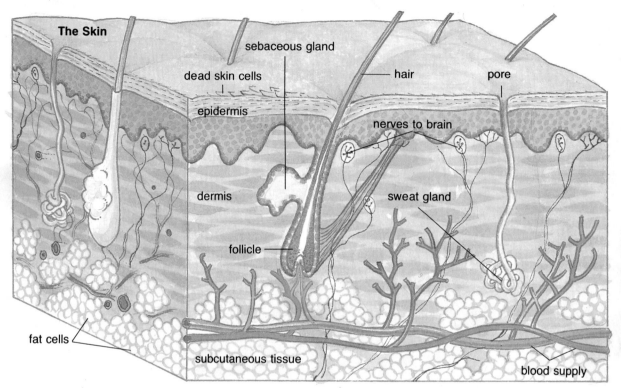

The Skin

sebaceous gland

dead skin cells — hair — pore

epidermis

nerves to brain

dermis — sweat gland

follicle

fat cells

subcutaneous tissue — blood supply

Your skin is made up of layers of tiny **cells,** packed closely together. The top layer, the **epidermis** has dead skin cells that rub off all the time. New cells are always forming inside your skin.

The lower layer or **dermis** has **nerve** cells that send messages to your brain, and **sweat glands** that lead to tiny holes in the skin called **pores.**

Hair **follicles** in the dermis hold the roots of each hair. **Sebaceous glands** in the dermis make an oil that protects the skin and hair.

   A child has a smooth, elastic skin that moves back easily when stretched. An old person's skin has many folds and wrinkles, especially on the face.

in old age, skin fits the body less tightly

What Skin Does

The boxer in the picture is sweating
from hitting the punching bag.
He feels hot and is red in the face.
The redness of his skin is caused by
blood rushing to his face. The extra
heat from the warm blood passes
through his skin. This helps him to
cool down.

When you sweat, the water in the
sweat **evaporates,** which also makes
your skin cooler.

a cat's fur feels soft

The sense of feeling in
your skin helps your body
to recognize many signals.
When you touch something,
nerves in your skin tell
your brain if the object
is hot or cold, soft or hard.
If you cut or scrape
yourself, the nerves also
tell your brain that you
are hurt and need help.

**the brain gets pain
messages from the skin**

Skin Color

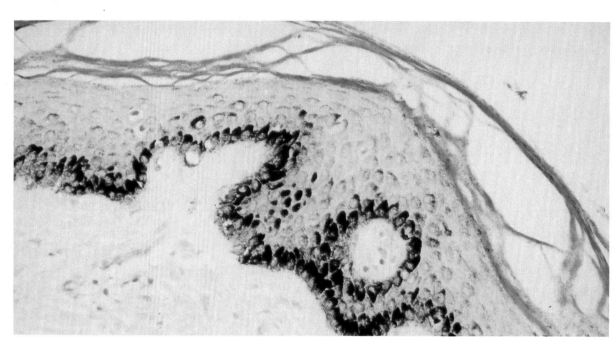

People throughout the world have skins of different colors.
Skin color helps protect the body from harmful **ultraviolet rays** which come from the sun.

The epidermis contains a dark-colored **pigment** called **melanin.** Melanin soaks up the ultraviolet rays. The photograph of some skin, taken under a microscope, shows a layer of dark spots of melanin.

this boy's skin has a lot
of the pigment melanin

People with pale skins turn darker in the sun. Their bodies produce extra melanin to protect them from the ultraviolet rays.

Freckles and moles are parts of the skin that have more melanin in them and so are darker.

Some people who have yellowish skins have more of the pigment **carotene** in the dermis.

this boy has the pigment carotene in his skin

this girl has a pale skin with little pigment in it

New Skin for Old

If you look at a cut or wound through a microscope, you can see a network of thin strands of **fibrin** trapping the blood cells to make the blood **clot.** The blood dries, and then a solid **scab** forms over the wound to stop dirt and **germs** from getting into your body while the new skin is growing. In the picture, the red blood cells are colored yellow for you to see them.

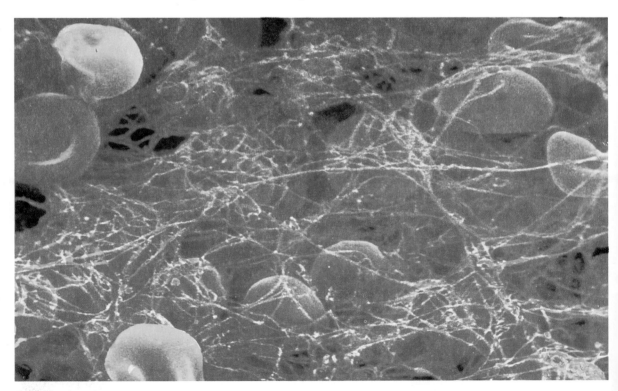

a scar from a bad cut

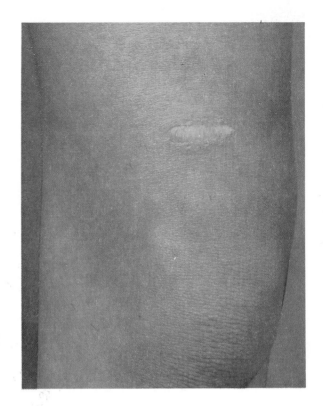

If a cut only breaks the epidermis, then it will not leave a mark or scar when it heals.

If someone has a very deep skin wound or a bad burn, doctors may replace the damaged skin with a **skin graft.** The wound then heals well, without leaving any scar.

serious fires can cause bad injuries

Taking Care of the Skin

You should take care of your skin and keep it healthy. Damaged skin makes it easy for germs to get into the body. Dirty skin will let germs grow. Eating lots of fruit and vegetables helps to keep your skin healthy. It is also important to drink lots of water and other liquids such as fruit juices or milk.

**washing
keeps your
skin clean**

You should wash regularly to keep your skin free of oil, dirt, germs, and dead skin cells. Sometimes, plugs of **sebum** from your sebaceous glands block your pores. These plugs of sebum appear as **blackheads.**

**too much sun can
be bad for you, so use a
sunscreen to protect your skin**

17

Skin Problems

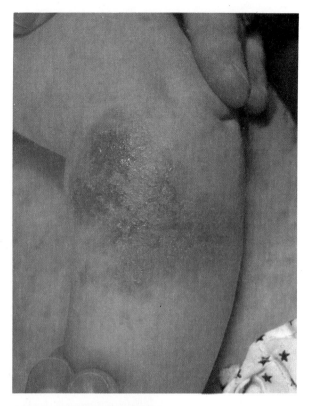

Damaged cells can make your skin red and itchy. This child has **eczema** and her arm has become blistered and sore.

Itching can also be caused by **parasites** such as lice and fleas which suck blood from the skin.

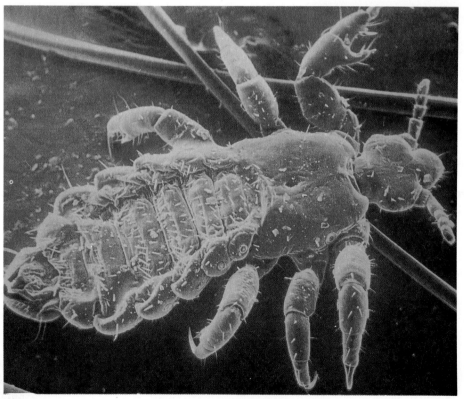

a microscope shows this head louse clinging to human hair

Dermatitis is an itchy red rash or patch of spots on the skin.
It may be caused by an **allergy** to something you have touched or eaten.

Some **infectious diseases** such as measles may also show on the skin.

The baby in the picture has a bad case of chicken pox. His skin is covered in itchy spots that will later become blisters and scabs. His brother has already had the disease and cannot catch it again.

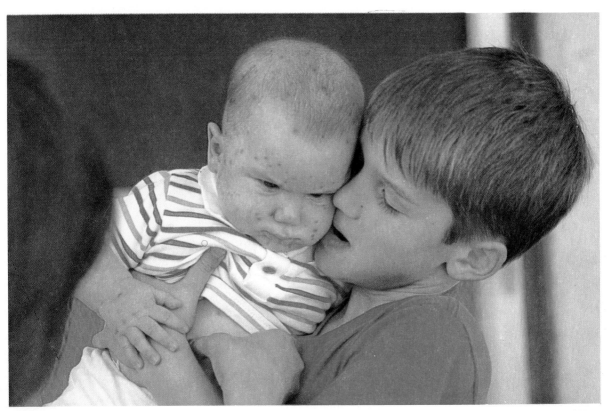

Our Nails

Nails protect the ends of your fingers and toes. They grow from a deep fold in the skin and are made of a thick layer of **keratin,** a material that does not break easily. The skin beneath the nail covers the **quick,** the living root of the nail.

This is the inside of a finger. The finger bone is in the center, with fatty tissue around it. Skin lies on top of the tissue, and the nail plate grows from a deep fold in the skin. A toenail grows in the same way.

nail bed

skin

fold in skin

nail plate

bone   fatty tissue

quick

your nails protect your finger tips

20

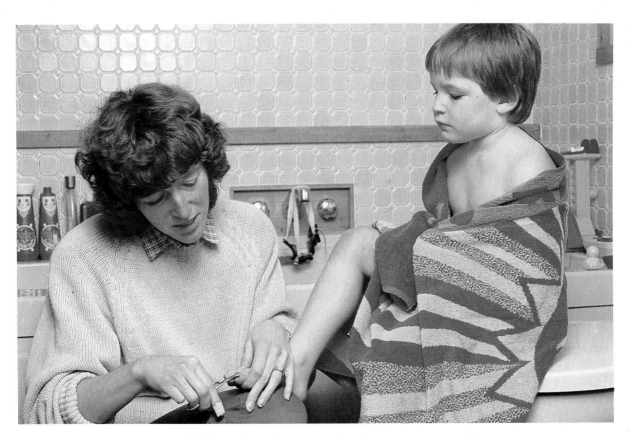

Your nails help protect the **sensitive** tips of your fingers and toes. There are over 1,000 nerve endings in one square inch of a fingertip. Fingernails also make the ends of our fingers firm so we can pick things up.

It is important to take care of your nails because a broken or injured nail can be very painful. Trim your nails regularly and keep them clean by scrubbing them with a nail brush when you wash your hands.

Why Do We Have Hair?

Your hair helps to keep you warm because it stops some heat from leaving your body through the head. Young babies have very little hair. Many men lose their hair as they grow older.

By the time the baby in the picture has his third birthday, he will have a full head of hair.

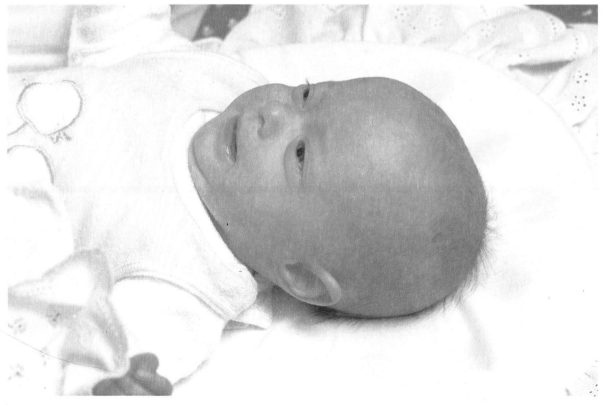

At **puberty,** children grow thicker hair on their arms and legs, in their armpits, and in the pubic region between the legs.

As boys become men, they grow hair on their face. Many shave this hair off because they do not want a beard or mustache. Men may also grow a lot of hair on the chest and back.

This man is bald because **hormones** in his body have made his hair fall out.

these Sikh men wear beards as part of their religion

How Hair Grows

You have about 100,000 hairs on your head. All are made from keratin.

Each hair has its root in a hair follicle in the dermis of the skin. The shape of the follicle forms the type of hair. A straight shaft of hair grows from a round follicle. If the follicle is oval, the shaft bends to form wavy hair. A curly shaft of hair grows from a flat follicle.

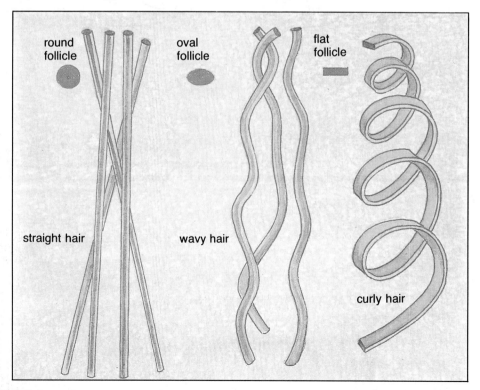

round follicle

oval follicle

flat follicle

straight hair

wavy hair

curly hair

Hair Color

Your hair color is usually like that of your parents or grandparents. If your **ancestors** came from Africa, your hair is likely to be black because of the pigment melanin in it and curly.

this brother and sister have the same wavy, red hair

People from Asia often have straight black hair. In Northern Europe many people have blond or red hair that is straight or wavy.

The color of your hair depends on which pigments you have in your skin and how much of each pigment there is.

As people become older, their hair turns white because their bodies no longer make pigment to color their hair.

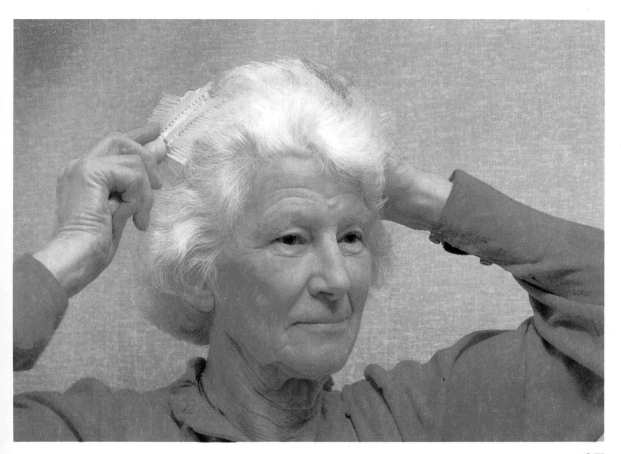

Hair Care

One of the most common problems people have with their hair is dandruff. This is dead skin that flakes off the scalp.

You should wash your hair regularly, especially if you live in a city. Avoid using a shampoo that is too strong, and rinse your hair very well. If you use a blow dryer, don't set it too hot as heat can damage hair.

Comb and brush your hair gently and do not tug at it.

The **magnified** photo shows how the scales of keratin on a shaft of hair overlap each other. Shafts of healthy hair are smooth and unbroken. Split ends may be caused by rough treatment. They will not mend, and need to be cut off.

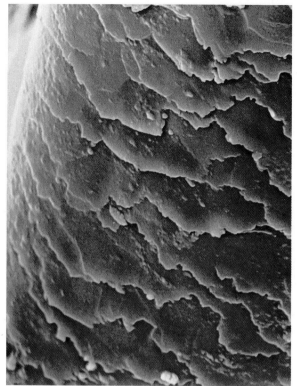

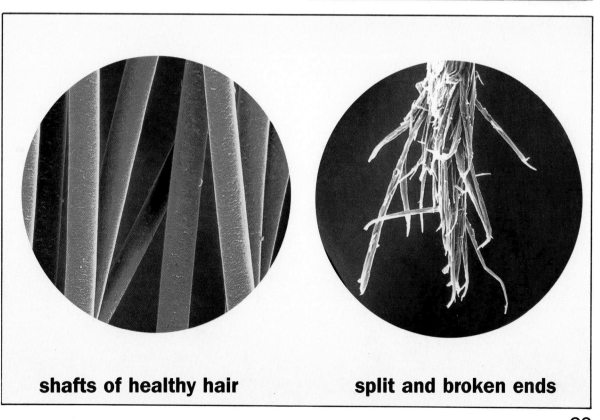

shafts of healthy hair　　　**split and broken ends**

Our Teeth

Newborn babies do not
have any teeth. By the
time a child is two, the
milk teeth have grown.
These fall out at about the
age of five or six and are
replaced by the teeth you
keep for the rest of your
life.

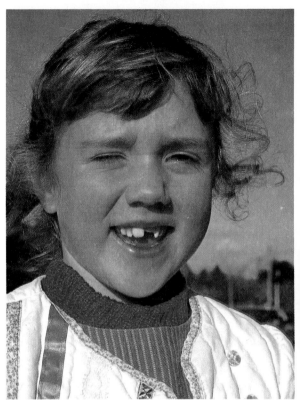

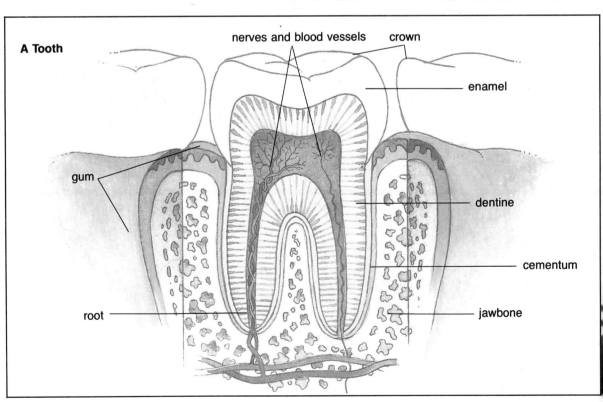

A Tooth

nerves and blood vessels

crown

enamel

gum

dentine

cementum

root

jawbone

The part of the tooth you can see, the **crown,** is covered with a hard **enamel** which makes the tooth strong and protects it from germs. Under the enamel is a layer of **dentine** which surrounds the nerves and **blood vessels** in the **pulp.** The root, which is covered by a bony layer of **cementum,** fixes the tooth firmly into the **jawbone.**

Without teeth we would find it difficult to bite and chew hard foods.

chewing hard food like a stalk of celery helps keep your teeth healthy

Taking Care of Our Teeth

If you do not brush your teeth properly, a coating of millions of germs called plaque grows on the surface of your teeth. These germs make an **acid** as they feed on the bits of food in the mouth. The acid attacks the tooth enamel and causes **decay.** It makes a hole, or cavity, in the tooth.

You can use special tablets to stain the plaque red and see the places you have missed when brushing your teeth.

The best way to avoid tooth decay is to clean your teeth properly, and to visit your dentist regularly.

Brush your teeth for three minutes every time you clean them. You could use an egg timer to check.

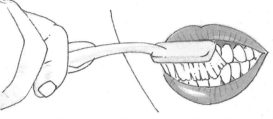

1. Brush the top teeth downward from the gums, not forgetting the back teeth.

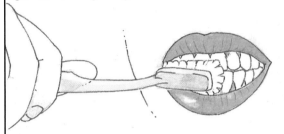

2. Then brush the bottom teeth upward in the same way.

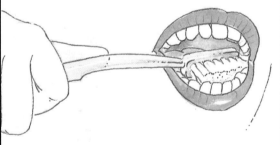

3. Brush the backs of the top teeth and the backs of the bottom teeth.

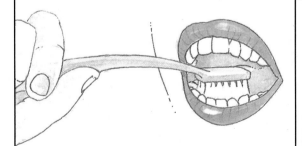

4. Brush the biting surfaces of all the teeth, top and bottom.

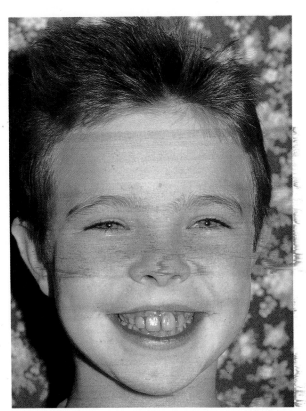

red dye stains the plaque

Eating too much sweet food is very bad for your teeth. If you do eat sugary foods, clean your teeth carefully afterward.

Cheese, milk, and green vegetables contain **calcium** which helps keep your bones and teeth hard. Chewing hard food keeps your teeth healthy, too.

Going to the Dentist

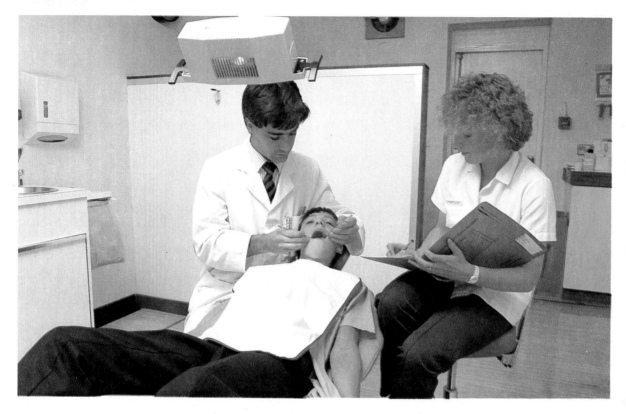

Regular visits to the dentist help to
stop you from getting cavities.
You should have a checkup every six
months so that the dentist can make
sure your teeth are all right.
The dentist looks at each tooth using
a little mirror to see the backs, and
a **probe** to get rid of any bits of
food stuck between your teeth.

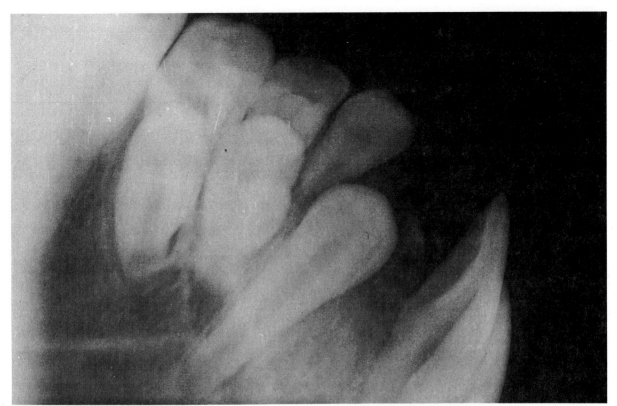

an X-ray photograph

The dentist can take an
X ray of your teeth to
find out whether there is
any decay inside the tooth.
If there is a cavity, the
dentist will first give
you an **injection** to stop
any pain, and then will
cut out the decay and fill
the hole with **amalgam.**

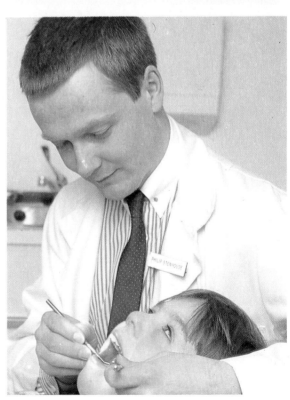

a dentist using a mirror

Dental Work

If all a person's teeth are missing, the dentist replaces them with a full set of false teeth or dentures. An **impression** is made of the patient's mouth, then the dental technician takes care to make sure that the new dentures fit well.

this model shows how a bridge is used to fix a false crown in position

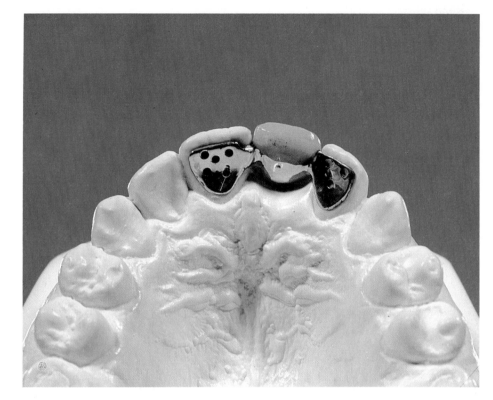

If only one tooth is missing, the dentist may replace it with a false tooth and use a bridge to fix the new tooth to the teeth on either side.

If your teeth are crooked, an **orthodontist** may make you a special **brace** which will gradually straighten the teeth.

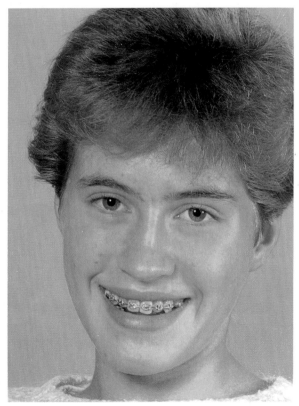

wearing braces

How We Look

The way you look affects the way people think about you. Many people use makeup to improve their appearance, and they change the style and color of their hair. Some people, like clowns, use makeup to show us how they are feeling. A funny face can make us laugh, but a sad face makes us feel sorry for the clown.

Young people often try new styles that shock older people. It can be fun to try out different styles, but too many strong chemicals may damage the hair.
Makeup must be removed properly after use or it may block the pores and cause skin problems.

boys in Thailand who become Buddhist monks have their heads shaved

some people wear strange hairstyles and makeup

Keeping Well Groomed

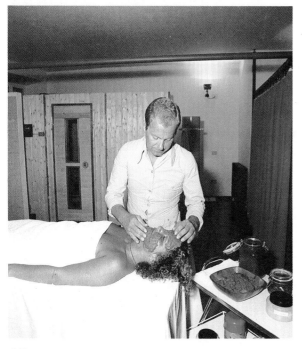

People have different ways of keeping their skin, hair, and nails in good condition.

In traditional Japanese baths, people soap and rinse themselves before plunging into the water.

Some people use a face mask of herbs or mud to help beautify their skin.

Saunas and steam baths help to clean the skin by making the body sweat. The pores in the skin open, and as the sweat runs from the body, the dirt is washed away.

Gentle **massage** is good for the skin and helps a person to relax.

Washing your hair often with a mild shampoo keeps it clean and healthy.

The manicurist in the picture is applying nail polish to a woman's fingernails. The nails have been filed and cleaned to make them attractive.

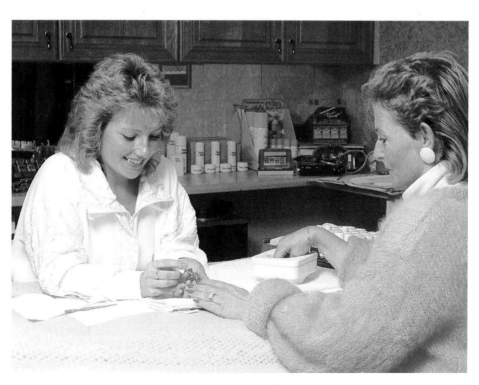

a manicurist at work

Accidents

the steam from a kettle can burn the skin badly

cool the burn off quickly by putting it under cold running water

cover the burn loosely with a clean, dry cloth

When there is an accident, stay calm and call an adult right away. You can sometimes help someone before help arrives, but you must know exactly what to do. Groups like the Red Cross run courses to teach people first aid.

Large burns, wounds, and other injuries must be treated by a doctor.

take a bee sting out carefully with tweezers

press a pack of ice in a cloth over the sting to stop the pain and reduce the swelling

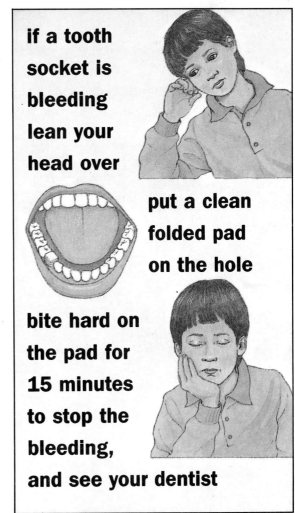

if a tooth socket is bleeding lean your head over

put a clean folded pad on the hole

bite hard on the pad for 15 minutes to stop the bleeding, and see your dentist

If an animal bites you, you must always see a doctor. The doctor may give you an injection against any infectious disease the animal might give you.

If you get a splinter, ask someone to pull it out with clean tweezers.

Do not break a blister. It will heal better on its own.

43

Some Skin, Hair, and Nails Facts

The photograph of some human skin taken under a microscope shows the epidermis colored in red, and the dermis in blue. The blood cells in the dermis are also colored in red.

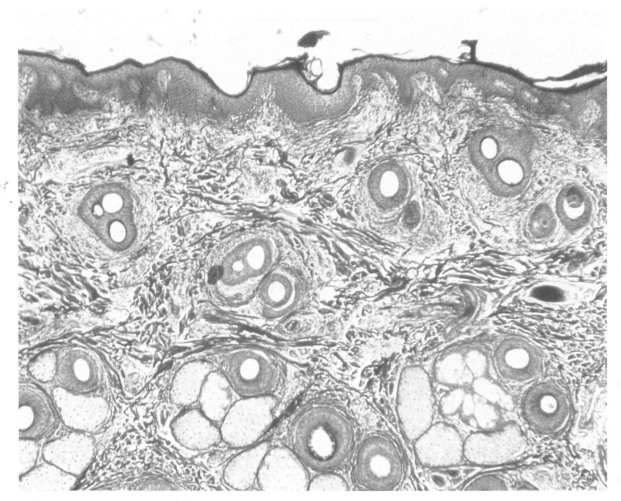

About 200 years ago people wore such tall wigs that mice were sometimes found nesting in them!

The longest head hair recorded was 26 feet long and the longest thumbnail was 33 inches long.

Murari Aditya holds the world record for the longest fingernails. It took 25 years for the nails of his left hand to reach a length of 120 in.

Murari Aditya after cutting his fingernails

Glossary

acid a strong, sour substance that eats away solid things.

allergy an illness caused when something such as dust has an unusual effect on the body.

amalgam a mixture of metals used to fill a cavity in a tooth.

ancestor a relative who lived and died a long time ago.

blackhead a plug of oil with a black head that blocks a pore in the skin.

blood vessels tubes that carry blood around your body.

brace a set of wires worn in the mouth to straighten teeth.

bridge a false tooth that is kept in the mouth by being fixed to the real teeth.

calcium a substance found in green leafy vegetables and dairy foods needed for healthy bones, teeth, and muscles.

carotene an orange-red coloring found in many plants and in humans.

cell a very small part or unit.

cementum a thin bone-like material that covers the outside of the root of a tooth.

clot when parts of a liquid such as blood join together so that it stops flowing.

crown the top part of a tooth that shows above the gums.

decay to waste or rot away.

dentine a yellow layer of tooth under the hard outer coating.

dermis the layer of skin beneath the outside layer.

eczema a condition that makes skin red, flaky, and itchy.

enamel the hard surface of the tooth containing calcium.

epidermis the top skin layer.

evaporate to change from a liquid into a gas.

fibrin a substance in the blood that helps the blood thicken so it cannot flow out of a cut.

follicles small channels in the skin from which hairs grow.

germ a tiny living thing that can cause disease.

hormone a substance made in the body that triggers changes such as growth.

impression an imprint of an object made in something soft. Impressions of teeth and the shape of the jaw area are made in wax or plaster and then used to make dentures.

infectious disease an illness that can be caught from other people or animals.

injection a way of putting

medicine very quickly into the body through a needle pushed into the skin.

jawbone   the hinged lower bone of your mouth that makes your chin.

keratin   the tough substance in your hair and nails. The surface of your skin is also covered with keratin.

magnified   when something is made to look larger.

massage   gentle stroking and rubbing of skin and muscles.

melanin   a black or dark brown coloring substance found in skin and hair.

microscope   an instrument that makes tiny things look larger.

milk teeth   the first set of teeth that a child grows.

nerves   a network of tiny "cables" that pass messages from all parts of the body to the brain and back again.

orthodontist   a dentist who can give treatment to make teeth grow straight and even.

parasite   a tiny creature that lives on another animal or human body.

pigment   a substance in plants or animals that gives the color to leaves, fur, hair, or skin.

pore   a tiny hole in your skin.

probe   a tool used by a dentist to get bits of food out of your teeth and to find holes that need filling.

puberty   the age when a child's body becomes an adult body.

pulp   the soft center of a tooth.

quick   any area of skin that feels pain or touch very easily, especially underneath a nail.

sauna   a bath of hot water poured over heated stones to make steam. The steam cleanses the skin.

scab   the covering built up in layers over a cut.

sebaceous glands   glands in the dermis that make an oil that protects and covers the skin and hair.

sebum   an oil that protects and covers the skin and hair.

sensitive   describes something that reacts quickly to touch or pain.

skin graft   treating burns and bad wounds by taking skin from another part of the body to cover the damaged area.

sweat glands   pockets in the skin that produce sweat.

ultraviolet ray   invisible rays from the sun. We need these rays to stay healthy, but too much of them is harmful.

X ray   a ray that can see through solid objects.

Index

© Heinemann Children's Reference 1990
Artwork © BLA Publishing Limited 1987

Material used in this book first appeared in Macmillan World Library: HOW OUR BODIES WORK: Skin, Hair and Teeth. Published by Heinemann Children's Reference

Photographic credits
(t = top b = bottom l = left r = right)
cover: © Kozlowski/FPG; 4 Camilla Jessell Photo Library; 5t, 5b Frank Lane Picture Agency; 6t Bridgeman Art Library; 6b Ancient Art and Architecture Collection; 7 Science Photo Library; 9t, 9b Trevor Hill; 10 Sporting Pictures; 11t, 11b Trevor Hill; 12 Science Photo Library; 13t, 13bl, 13br Trevor Hill; 14 Science Photo Library; 15t Trevor Hill; 15b Rex Features; 16, 17t Trevor Hill; 17b J. Allan Cash; 18 St Bartholomew's Hospital; 18b Science Photo Library; 19 S. & R. Greenhill; 20, 21, 22, 23t Trevor Hill; 23 J. Allan Cash; 25 Trevor Hill; 26t J. Allan Cash; 26b Camilla Jessell Photo Library; 27, 28 Trevor Hill; 29t, 29bl, 29br Science Photo Library; 30, 31, 33t, 33b, 34, 35t, 35b, 36 Trevor Hill; 37t Science Photo Library; 37b Trevor Hill; 38 J. Allan Cash; 39t ZEFA; 39b S. & R. Greenhill; 40t Japanese Tourist Office; 40b J. Allan Cash; 41 Trevor Hill; 44 Science Photo Library; 45t Mary Evans Picture Library; 45b Frank Spooner Pictures